T0198842

THE PRACTICAL STRATEGIES SERIES
IN GIFTED EDUCATION

series editors
FRANCES A. KARNES & KRISTEN R. STEPHENS

Inventions and Inventing for Gifted Students

Thomas P. Hébert

Routledge
Taylor & Francis Group

NEW YORK AND LONDON

First published 2005 by Prufrock Press Inc.

Published 2021 by Routledge
605 Third Avenue, New York, NY 10017
2 Park Square, Milton Park, Abingdon, Oxon OX14 4RN

Routledge is an imprint of the Taylor & Francis Group, an informa business

ISBN 13: 978-1-59363-175-8 (pbk)

Contents

The Practical Strategies Series in Gifted Education offers teachers, counselors, administrators, parents, and other interested parties up-to-date instructional techniques and information on a variety of issues pertinent to the field of gifted education. Each guide addresses a focused topic and is written by scholars with authority on the issue. Several guides have been published. Among the titles are:

- *Acceleration Strategies for Teaching Gifted Learners*
- *Curriculum Compacting: An Easy Start to Differentiating for High-Potential Students*
- *Enrichment Opportunities for Gifted Learners*
- *Independent Study for Gifted Learners*
- *Motivating Gifted Students*
- *Questioning Strategies for Teaching the Gifted*
- *Social & Emotional Teaching Strategies*
- *Using Media & Technology With Gifted Learners*

For a current listing of available guides within the series, please contact Prufrock Press at (800) 998-2208 or visit http://www.prufrock.com.

Invention is "a source of hope that life will be better tomorrow compared to today; invention is the key to solving many of the problems we face."
—M. Hertz (1999, p. 101)

During my first year as a teacher of gifted students, I met a young inventor named Jonathan. He arrived in my classroom and proudly announced that he had a great idea for an independent project. He explained to me that, as far back as he could remember, he had watched his father suffer from severe backaches and was concerned about his dad every week when it was time to mow the family's lawn. Jonathan was currently a fourth grader, and as he shared his worries about his father, he claimed that, as a kindergarten student, he had vowed to do something to help his dad.

With this promise to his father in mind, Jonathan decided to address his dad's problem through an invention. He announced that he had plans to design a pair of shoes that would incorporate tiny mowers underneath the soles, enabling his father to wear them and simply walk across the family's grass as the tiny lawn mower shoes trimmed the grass. Jonathan began working in my classroom on sophisticated blueprints for his invention. In a short time, he had acquired a collection of used shoes from the teachers in our elementary school. He was completely absorbed in his project as he worked on attaching a tiny lawn mower engine underneath the soles of the wing-tip shoes he had managed to elevate with pieces of lumber.

Jonathan's friends were delighted when he presented his final product, "Lawn Mower Shoes," and began working on an advertising campaign to convince his neighbors and friends to invest in his new product. While Jonathan was working on his advertisements, the young women in Jonathan's fourth-grade class quickly pointed out that his wing-tip prototype was somewhat sexist. As a result, Jonathan proceeded to design the feminine version of the "Lawn Mower Shoes." Within a week, he created a women's open-toed, high-heeled sandal that was also equipped with a built-in mower. Jonathan was ready to convince both men and women in his community that "Lawn Mower Shoes" were the answer to every suburban homeowner's drudgery.

Jonathan inspired me as a teacher. His experiences in the classroom helped me realize how much fun young people could have with learning the inventing process while simultaneously developing their creative thinking skills. From then on, teaching inventions became a standard component of my curriculum.

Several years after my work with Jonathan, I taught gifted students in the Department of Defense Dependents Schools in West Germany and enjoyed working with families of the military. Following a unit I taught on inventing, Jack, a highly creative middle school student, won first prize in our classroom Invention Convention with a simple gadget he created to solve a pet peeve he faced quite often.

Jack explained that his family enjoyed dining out in quaint, rustic restaurants in their travels throughout the German countryside. He noted that the tables in these restaurants were often rather wobbly and needed to be steadied. Since Jack did not want to appear rude and trouble the waiters and waitresses, he designed a small block of wood in which he carved four different corners with varying levels of height. He attached rubberized material to the bottom of the block to insure that his gadget would remain in place. With his pocket-sized contraption, Jack and his family could quietly slip his "Trusty Table Steadier" under a wobbly leg and maintain a steady table, as well as prevent any embarrassment for his American family living overseas.

My students at the University of Alabama enjoyed the same challenge of solving a pet peeve or "bug" in a course entitled Fostering Creative Expression. Susan, an elementary education major, was involved in clinical field experiences in which she spent time in local elementary schools working with young children. With the winter colds that ran rampant throughout the elementary school, Susan noticed that teachers constantly had to supervise students as they walked to and from the classroom tissue box. As she observed the sniffling students, she came up with a clever idea for an invention with great appeal to elementary educators. She chose to wear a roll of toilet tissue hanging from her neck. She strung the roll of tissue through a colorful, wide ribbon decorated with fancy rhinestones and beads she acquired at a craft store and proudly wore her handy new necklace. As she walked around the elementary classroom throughout the day, she was able to deliver the badly needed tissue to sniffily students at their desks, and soon classroom traffic to the tissue box ceased.

Kristie, a doctoral student at the University of Georgia, confessed to her colleagues in my graduate creativity class that she badly needed a shot of caffeine to jump-start her day. Kristie explained that she needed the caffeine that coffee provided in the morning, yet she wanted to begin her day with a more nutritional alternative. Kristie experienced her "Aha!" in the middle of the grocery store when she discovered bottles of caffeinated water on the shelf. She promptly purchased several bottles and used it in making her morning orange juice from concentrate. By combining her healthy fruit juice concentrate with the caffeinated water, she had the morning jump-start she wanted and was able to maintain the nutritional nourishment she needed in her hectic graduate-school lifestyle. She called her caffeinated orange juice "Orange Jounce," and her advertising campaign included her slogan "Orange Jounce: It's Nutrition With an Attitude!"

What did Jonathan, Jack, Susan, and Kristie have in common? They all solved a personal problem—a "bug" or a pet peeve—with a clever invention. In addition, they had an enjoyable time with the process and developed their creative thinking skills through designing inventions. Students of any age can benefit from the invention experience and may spend hours of enjoyment looking around their environment and coming up with all kinds of great ways to make life a little easier for themselves and their families.

Why Teach Inventing?

Creativity researchers and theorists indicate that inventing involves creativity applied to a problem-solving process, which can be taught. The cognitive thought processes for increasing creativity, problem solving, and generating innovative ideas can be developed through instruction and systematically directed and applied to a school curriculum (Cramond, 2005; Davis, 2005; Halpern, 1996; Torrance & Safter, 1999). Educators who are dedicated to delivering thinking skills instruction appreciate being able to offer cognitive training to students.

Through teaching instructional units on inventing, multiple creative thinking skills are infused into one unit. Teachers who provide their students with such instruction see inventions as a natural way of packaging creativity training in an authentic and meaningful way.

Proponents of thinking skills instruction have indicated that learning is more meaningful to young people if the skills they are being trained to master are embedded within the content of the curriculum (Halpern, 1996; Hester, 1994; Schlichter, 1997). Isolated activities in creativity skills simply do not carry the same long-lasting effects. Educators in gifted education have also argued that high-ability students are better served in school if they are provided opportunities to design original products that incorporate the application of creativity skills (Betts & Kercher, 1999; Feldhusen & Britton-Kolloff, 1986; Renzulli, 1999). Therefore, having students design original inventions as products is a pedagogically sound practice.

Before beginning instruction on inventing, teachers may want to consider ways in which they might entice their students to pursue the invention process.

Invite inventors in nearby communities as inspirational guest speakers in the classroom. These highly creative adults can discuss their inventive processes. Hearing from successful inventors helps to motivate students, as well as make them aware of the real challenges involved in the invention process.

Students may also enjoy field trips to museums that feature exhibits relating to inventions and inventing. Some states even host invention fairs where the creations of highly innovative young inventors throughout the state are on display. Seeing what other students are capable of designing often inspires students.

Interest Centers to Inspire Inventors

Many classroom teachers have motivated students to explore inventing by providing them with an interest development center in the classroom. Such a center might include newspaper articles about inventions, examples of weird and wacky inventions, feature stories from magazines on successful inventors, or crates of interesting junk with which students can experiment. The interest development center enables classroom teachers to continually provide new materials to stimulate interest in inventing.

Provide primary grade students with plastic buckets and boxes filled with colorful recyclable junk in a designated "Inventor's Corner" of the classroom. Empty bottles of window washing spray, plastic drinking straws, egg cartons, and many other "junkyard treasures" that normally end up in the trash can be connected or combined in a wild variety of ways to create prototypes of new bicycles, space stations, or toys for pet animals. These original contraptions that enthusiastic young students are delighted to invent can be given clever names and placed on display for visitors to the classroom or school to enjoy.

Classroom Collections of Books on Inventing

Along with interest centers filled with student resources and hands-on activities related to inventing, a classroom collection of books on inventions, inventors, and inventing helps to inspire students to become involved with inventing. A visit to the school's media center or the local public library can provide classroom teachers with a wealth of helpful resources.

Jim Murphy's (1978) *Weird and Wacky Inventions* is an entertaining collection of actual invention patent drawings from the past. Each page of the book provides the reader with hints at what the invention was designed to do. Most of the lesser-known inventions featured in the book may now be considered outlandish; however, with exposure to such inventions, students can be motivated to think of wonderful ideas for inventions of their own. For example, a class of middle school students became intrigued with two of Jim Murphy's inventions, which in turn inspired a morning of activity in the classroom. One group of students enjoyed field-testing prototypes of inventions they created that would allow individuals to eat grapefruit without splattering juice in their eyes. A second group had fun coming up with delightful new contraptions that enabled them to eat spaghetti easily and in creative ways. Since the publication of *Weird and Wacky Inventions*, a number of helpful resources on inventing have been published (see the Resources section).

In addition to enticing students to become involved in inventing, helping students become aware of inventors and the stories of inventions is also important. Beginning a curricular unit with a historical perspective of inventors and their innovations is useful. Young inventors should be aware of the many creative and innovative thinkers and their significant role in shaping the world. As an introduction to inventing, students should think about how everyday conveniences are taken for granted. As Starko (2001) noted,

> It is easy to go through life assuming that Scotch tape or facial tissues or drinking straws always existed. If we were questioned, probably most of us would realize that those ideas must have come from somewhere, but it is easy to forget that all objects that fill our lives, from paper clips to computer chips, are the product of someone's new idea. Someone had to ask, "What is needed here?" "What is the problem here?" or "How could this be better?" (pp. 224–225)

Having students examine problems and determine what can be undertaken to make things better can be facilitated through a little fun with history. Some students become fascinated with inventions historically, and books describing the emergence of inventions over time may inspire their fascination. Many of these resources are encyclopedia-like in style and provide students with colorful illustrations of intriguing contraptions and inventions that have changed the way we live (see the Resources section). In addition, some students become fascinated with the stories of the inventors and the process they pursued in developing their innovations. Consider sharing vignettes about inventors and their inventions with students to nurture this interest.

Children's literature may also serve to inspire potential young inventors. Children's picture books featuring inventions can captivate creative youngsters and get them to begin considering their own talents as problem solvers, invention designers, and young entrepreneurs. E. L. Konigsburg's (1991) *Samuel Todd's Book of Great Inventions* is a delightful picture book that highlights simple inventions that young children use every day. The reader spends a day with a young boy named Samuel Todd and through his eyes experiences the wealth of inventions—from Velcro sneakers and ski parkas, to school backpacks—that shape the daily adventures of young children. Picture books such as Konigsburg's can serve as great introductions to instruction on inventing for primary grade students. With a little exploration through annotated directories of children's literature, educators will discover rich collections of stories centered on inventing and young inventors that will help build student interest.

An instructional unit on inventing and inventions would be incomplete without introducing students to the work of Rube Goldberg, whose invention cartoons captivated Americans for much of the 20th century as they poked fun at society's inefficient ways to solve simple problems. Although it may require a trip to a public library to acquire this book, which is no longer in print, Goldberg's (1979) *The Best of Rube Goldberg* is a wonderful collection of illustrations accompanied by step-by-step instructions that explain the ingenious, outlandish, as well as detailed and elaborate mechanical inventions Goldberg created for self-shining shoes, a self-operating corkscrew, and many others. Youngsters typically become enthralled with Goldberg's cartoons and beg teachers for time to illustrate their own whimsical versions of problem-solving devices in the spirit of Goldberg.

Invention Games

In addition to books about inventions and inventing, invention scavenger hunts may also help to motivate young inventors. Included in Westberg's (2002) menu of suggestions for enticing students to pursue inventing is her recommendation that teachers play a game in which small groups of three to four students take a walking tour of their school building and search for as many inventions as they can find. The teams of students receive one point for each of the inventions they spot. Once the teams have reported their invention hunt results, the class can enjoy a discussion concerning a few of the items on their lists. The teacher then poses questions such as

- Why was it invented?

- How does it work?

- Did a similar object exist in the past?

- How is this invention important to you?

This debriefing discussion is designed to create a new awareness of inventions in our world and get students thinking about the exciting possibilities of solving real problems in their own lives through inventing.

Flack's (1989) definitive book on teaching inventions in the classroom is another good resource. Several clever strategies Flack described can be adapted for use in the classroom, particularly for helping students to consider the thinking skills involved in the inventing process. For example, students can be divided into teams of four and each team provided with a box of dry spaghetti, a roll of scotch tape, and a raw egg. Students are then directed to use only the spaghetti and tape to build the tallest possible structure that holds the egg securely in place. As the teams work on their spaghetti structures, they should be instructed to pay close attention to all the mental processes they use as they work on the task. One group member can be selected as an observer and recorder to keep a record of the processes observed in the activity.

Following this type of activity, a debriefing regarding all the mental processes used in the act of inventing can be thoroughly discussed. From this discussion of "What mental activity went into the process of inventing?," students realize they incorporate observation, memory, trial and error, discovery, intuition, analysis, and evaluation into the invention process. Flack (1989) indicated that, in such an activity, students might enjoy debating the generated list of thinking skills they see in action; however, the important outcome of the activity is to have students understand that inventions unfold from complex cognitive processing. In addition, students enjoy thinking about the many ways inventors can solve a problem.

Share Examples of Other Young Inventors and Their Successes

Along with conducting invention games to generate interest in inventing, students benefit from seeing the work of other young people who enjoyed working on inventions in previous classes. As a teacher, make it a point to keep a camera in the classroom to capture the work of young inventors throughout their process. Each year, share these photos of previous classroom inventors and perhaps enshrine them in a "Classroom Inventors Hall of Fame."

Students often piggyback off the ideas of other students. One child's creativity often helps to spark the imagination of other young inventors. For example, when I shared Jonathan's "Lawn Mower Shoes" with students years after Jonathan had moved on to middle school, another young man followed with "Sticky Cinema Sweepers," a pair of shoes that incorporated rotating scrubbing brushes to clean the movie theater floor of sticky spilled soft drinks, popcorn, and candy. Another student named Paula created shoes designed to help her parents polish the kitchen floor. She attached buffing material to the bottom of her sneakers to create "Paula's Polishing Shoes." Thus, teachers should share many examples of student inventions from previous years, for the possibilities that may evolve are endless.

Descriptions of teaching the process of invention to children has remained consistent in the literature throughout the years (Caney, 1985; Erlbach, 1997; Flack, 1989; Shlesinger, 1987; Sobey, 1996; Starko, 2001; Taylor, 1987; Westberg, 1998). Whether students are designing inventions for competitive programs or building inventions to overcome an irritant in their lives, the basic steps they undergo are the same.

A modified approach of the process described in Steven Caney's (1985) *Invention Book* is recommended here for use in the classroom. Caney's work takes young inventors through the steps of coming up with good ideas for inventions, gathering materials for an inventor's workshop, building prototypes of inventions, field-testing inventions, and creating names for inventions, plus record-keeping, planning, and marketing the final product. This approach can be simplified into six stages: (1) awareness, (2) identifying a problem, (3) generating possibilities, (4) planning, (5) building, and (6) selling the idea. This simplified version of Caney's process enables teachers to teach the invention process in a classroom setting efficiently within a quarter of the school year.

Stage 1: Awareness

During the awareness stage, the introductory activities described previously motivate students to become involved in the process of inventing by creating an awareness of the importance of inventions in our daily lives and how they address everyday problems. Through activities such as listening to guest speakers, taking field trips to museums, reading books on inventing, working in interest centers, and tinkering with junk at the inventor's corner, students become aware of the importance of inventions and even more excited about the possibilities.

Stage 2: Identifying the Problem to be Solved

The second phase of instruction involves helping students to become cognizant of problems in their lives and getting them to consider the possibilities and opportunities around them. Have students generate a long list of problems, annoyances, or personal pet peeves. Each day, as a class, openly discuss these pet peeves and life annoyances, adding to the list as needed. Whether it is a family member who squeezes the tube of toothpaste incorrectly, tangled coat hangers in closets, or moviegoers who disturb others during a film, students are always able to think of many issues that aggravate or annoy them.

As students commiserate with each other, they continue to generate more ideas. Students should understand that they are expected to continue generating ideas at home and add more bugs to their lists whenever they think of new ones. Emphasize to students that, the longer their list of bugs, the easier it will be to eventually think of an idea for an invention.

Students should keep an "Inventor's Notebook" to organize their work. The list generated by each student can be the first entry into this notebook. Each time the class brainstorms, new ideas and lists can be added to the notebook.

Stage 3: Exploring the Possibilities

When students reach a point of saturation with their bug lists, it is time to move to the third stage, where they will begin to explore possible solutions to their problems. Once the problem is identified, the young inventor has to explore all the possibilities. It is the teacher's job to train students in as many divergent thinking techniques as possible to assist them in exploring the possibilities. SCAMPER, synectics, attribute listing, and random input are just a few of these techniques.

SCAMPER

When asking young inventors to think of many possibilities, the use of idea-generating questions will assist them in eliciting a generous list of diverse ideas. One of Osborn's (1961) recommendations for encouraging more divergent thinking in young people was to present them with questions that would invoke many ideas.

Eberle (1982) incorporated a number of creativity techniques for improving divergent thinking suggested by Osborn into a convenient acronym, SCAMPER (Substitute, Combine, Adapt, Modify, Minify or Magnify, Put to Other Uses, Eliminate or Elaborate, Reverse or Rearrange), which can easily be taught to young inventors. Eberle (1996) maintained that "knowledge recalled is subject to adaptation, combination, or other intellectual operations that serve to produce creative ideas" (p. 5). He indicated that the process of creative imagination involves rearranging or manipulating information drawn from memory, and he proposed a checklist technique he calls SCAMPER to generate creative ideas.

SCAMPER presents questions or suggestions that prompt and stimulate an individual to think creatively. Since the acronym is easy to remember, it can help children and adults generate longer lists of different ideas. In teaching SCAMPER, many of the questions Starko (2001) and Westberg (1998) highlighted regarding Eberle's strategy can be used. They suggested prompts that enable educators to see how they can utilize simple, yet helpful questions embedded in the SCAMPER technique to facilitate more divergent thinking.

The S in SCAMPER calls for substituting. When discussing substitution in SCAMPER, a facilitator would ask questions such as "What could I use instead?" or "What other ingredients or materials might I consider?" Young inventors can appreciate the use of substitution when they consider products such as vegetarian burgers and hot dogs. A child working on the creation of a board game might substitute a bed sheet for the game board to allow life-size players to be positioned on the board.

The C in SCAMPER represents combinations. It requires that students consider questions such as "Are there two things that I might combine to come up with something new?" or "Which ideas can be mixed together?" Students understand that new products are often the result of combinations. For example, one young inventor was asked by her teacher to collate and staple sets of class papers. She found that her wrist became sore from having to pound on the stapler for long periods of time, so she solved her problem by combining the stapler with a tiny miniature pillow she attached with Velcro. The padding from the tiny pillow allowed her to staple for hours without pain or bruises. Her ingenuity solved a classroom problem through combination.

The A in SCAMPER stands for adaptation. In adapting, people change something that is known to address a problem. In applying this strategy to generate more ideas, a facilitator might ask, "How could we change or adapt this?" and "Could we imitate something else?" For example, a young woman who enjoyed eating dinner in front of the television noticed her mother's lap desk one evening and was inspired to adapt the idea to meet her needs as a TV junkie. She designed a foam rubber pillow with a carved indentation in which her dinner plate could rest snugly. With the foam rubber pillow placed comfortably and securely in her lap, she could get comfy on the family sofa with her pizza and not have dinner interrupt her favorite TV programs.

Modifications are represented by the *M* in SCAMPER. Modifications can involve a variety of meanings. Along with making slight changes in a product or idea, modification can also involve designing something much smaller through "minification" or much larger through "magnification." One example of modification that students can appreciate is changing the color of a product, such as the green ketchup that has appeared on the shelves of our grocery stores. Students readily understand how something is minified through examples of wristband televisions, cell phones, and bite-sized crackers and snacks. They also appreciate the value of magnifying something through examples like jumbo-sized sodas, extra-strength medicines, and large-screen TVs.

A young inventor using the *M* in SCAMPER decided to create a gigantic pair of plywood scissors to which he attached dusty chalkboard erasers. The boy suffered from asthma and was troubled every time his teacher asked him to go outside and clean out the chalkboard erasers by banging them against the brick school building. The dust involved in this classroom chore was more than he could handle, but with his enormous pair of scissors, he was able to clap the chalk dust out of the erasers without suffering breathing difficulty. Magnification helped to solve his problem.

The *P* in SCAMPER involves putting something to other uses. In facilitating this component, one might ask, "How might I use this in a new way?" For example, using sealable sandwich bags to pack neckties in luggage, using an antique dairy can to serve as a decorative umbrella holder, or using baby food jars to store a supply of screws, nails, and other hardware supplies.

The *E* in SCAMPER means eliminating something. Fat-free, carbohydrate-free, and sugar-free foods are something students hear about every day and are great examples of products involving elimination. In conducting SCAMPER, a teacher might ask, "What can be eliminated?" or "Is everything needed here?" Students examining how to make a child's school day more interesting might naturally respond with eliminating homework; however, a more serious discussion of that idea might lead to a teacher thinking about eliminating curricular requirements for students who prove mastery of the skills. SCAMPER may lead to curriculum compacting. Another example students can appreciate is stick-on translucent bookmarkers that enable readers to mark passages in a magazine or book, thus eliminating pen or pencil markings.

The final letter in SCAMPER calls for us to rearrange or reverse. Starko (2001) suggested using questions such as "Could I use a different sequence?," "Could I do the opposite?," and " What would happen if I turned it upside down, backward, or inside out?"(p. 178). Young inventors will recognize the value of this questioning when they think about reversible clothing and left-handed tools. They may also recognize the "rearrangement" in reusable magnetic calendars with months and dates that can be rearranged according to the number of days in each month.

Flack (1989), an avid proponent of SCAMPER, explained the importance of training young inventors in this technique in order to improve their products. He noted that,

> Anyone engaged in creative thinking, problem solving, and inventing can profit from a jump-start to get the brain fully functioning. In their creation of inventions, students should be habitually asking themselves how they can use the SCAMPER processes to improve existing products and to make their newest inventions even better. (p. 80)

To expose students to the many ways SCAMPER strategies might be used by inventors, consider sharing a collection of gadget catalogs, such as those typically found in the seat pocket of airplanes. Students enjoy perusing through these catalogs and become intrigued with many of the clever gadgets that are sold for expensive prices. For example, Christmas cookies for dogs that are decorated with green and red sugar sprinkles and contain garlic to ward off parasites, egg and vegetable shortening to help keep the dog's coat shiny, multiple grains to boost energy, and other healthy ingredients for building healthy dog tissue. Through the SCAMPER process, students can determine the questions inventors of such products asked themselves.

Synectics

Along with training in SCAMPER, students should receive instruction in synectics. Starko (2001) defined synectic methods as "metaphor- or analogy-based techniques for bringing elements together in search for new ideas or solutions" (p. 200). The essence of synectics, as proposed by the originators (Gordon & Poze, 1972), involves three metaphorical tools: personal analogy, compressed conflict, and direct analogy. Used by think tanks, research groups, and inventors, these synectic methods have been the stimulus behind many modern innovations.

When using personal analogy with young inventors, the goal is to have the problem solvers identify with some aspect of the problem in order to examine it in an unfamiliar way. In doing so, the student strives for an empathetic connection with the object or the problem posed. A young inventor attempting to create a new baby food serving dish might ask, "How would I feel if I were a dish used in feeding an infant child?" or "How might I enjoy looking different from other baby food serving dishes displayed in the department stores?" The student attempting to invent a new dish must attempt to create a personal involvement with the product.

Starko (2001) maintained that students' developmental levels combined with the amount of experience with personal analogies will influence the empathetic involvement in the analogies they produce. She indicated that, the greater the conceptual distance between the young inventor and the analogy, the greater the challenge is for him or her to reach empathetic involvement. Thus, personal analogies are both enjoyable and easy to use as prompts for problem-solving writing activities in students' Inventor's Notebooks. The following questions serve as examples:

- If you were the classroom's intercom speaker, how might you get more people to listen attentively to what you had to announce?

- If you were a school computer, how would you feel? How would you get students to treat you with more care?

Compressed conflicts, or symbolic analogies, are combinations of words that represent opposite ideas—oxymorons that appear self-contradictory (Davis, 2005). Compressed conflicts serve as a synectic technique by requiring one to think of two-word phrases that appear to conflict with one another and relate them to particular problems in order to stimulate original ideas. For example, "cautious speed" might be used by a school administrator to generate new ways of managing hundreds of children evacuating a school during a fire drill. "Tender durability" might represent the philosophical approach required to be successful in high school football.

Compressed conflicts serve as stretching exercises for young inventors. Just as athletes pursue daily physical stretching to prepare for athletic events, young inventors need mental stretching exercises to prepare them for their work as innovators. These practice exercises are not necessarily connected to any new content. They are simply infused into classroom discussions or writing activities in the Inventor's Notebooks to provide the youngsters with experiences of investigating the content of inventing from new perspectives.

The third synectic approach, direct analogy, offers additional thought-provoking ways to instruct students in the idea-generation and problem-solving phases of their inventive process. Flack (1989) claimed that direct analogies are the synectic technique that has the most direct bearing on inventing. Direct analogy is simply a comparison between two objects that share something in common. In direct analogies, a teacher asks students to look for parallels between two ideas, objects, or situations. Students will see similarities in form, function, or both when asked "How is a tree like a hat rack?" or " How are hairbrushes like porcupines?"

The power of direct analogies evolves when students are able to generate their own analogies that involve similarities between more remote objects. With more maturity in their abstract thinking, they become more adept at abstract thinking, which transfers to the creative process in designing inventions. For example, once young inventors have determined the problem they want to solve, they may, through direct analogy, search for situations in nature that are analogous to the problem they want to address: How does nature address similar problems? For example, ask students to imagine how bats, seagulls, polar bears, or kangaroos might have inspired inventors, designers, or engineers. Immersed in light-hearted discussion, students can suggest ways in which the behavior of animals might inspire inventors to think about solving problems.

Share examples of innovative products that evolved through analogous thinking with students. Young inventors are intrigued to hear how an engineer who spotted the clinging quality of cockleburrs, which clung to his pants when he walked through the fields, invented Velcro. They appreciate

Texture	Ingredients		Shape	Packaging
crunchy	almonds	granola	round	tissue paper
brittle	almonds	dried mangos	triangular	toy included
juicy	blueberries	peanuts	square	silver wrap
hard	oats	grape nuts	rectangular	rolled
crumbly	banana chips	apricots	sticks	edible paper
gooey	coconut	chocolate	tiny cubes	see-through

Figure 1. Brainstormed list for a health food bar

the analogy of camouflage fatigues being inspired by nature. They are intrigued that an inventive gentlemen who noticed that wet leaves falling from trees do not crumble like dry leaves led to the potatoes used for Pringles potato chips being sliced wet and then dried.

Attribute Listing

Another effective creativity strategy is attribute listing. Attribute listing is simple and efficient. Young inventors take whatever is the focus of concern and break it down into its most basic characteristics or component parts. They then think of all the possible values for each of the attributes. For example, a group of students might determine that a new recipe for a health food bar is needed that would appeal to their age group. They might consider the common attributes of health food bars: nutritious ingredients, rectangular shaped, wrapped in colorful cellophane, and chewy texture. The students then must consider the values of the attributes *texture, shape, nutritional ingredients*, and *packaging*.

Next, students should consider each attribute separately, generating brainstormed lists such as those presented in Figure 1. The process can result in a delicious treat made from a crunchy combination of dried banana chips, coconut, granola, and chocolate. The new treat might be shaped as triangles and wrapped in colorful, see-through foil, or it might be cube-shaped with morsels of blueberries, peanuts, and dried mangos wrapped in edible sugarcoated paper. Students can also generate clever names and catchy slogans to sell their newly invented products.

Random Input

Young inventors also enjoy using a strategy referred to as random input (de Bono, 1992). This technique promotes lateral thinking and the generation of innovative ideas. de Bono defined such thinking as "seeking to solve problems by unorthodox or apparently illogical methods" (p. 52). He maintained that educators could increase lateral thinking in their students through the systematic use of techniques that encourage alternative ways of thinking.

Starko (2001) explained random input as juxtaposing a problem or subject for creative thinking with a randomly selected word. She proposed that, by attempting to make connections between the problem and the unrelated word, students might be able to see the problem from a different perspective and generate many more ideas. Starko suggested that the classroom teacher should open a dictionary and randomly select a word. Since nouns are the most efficient sources of random input, if the word randomly selected is not a noun, continue down the alphabetical listing of words until you come to a noun.

For example, in applying this strategy to inventing, consider how students involved in thinking about designs for new school playground equipment might benefit from random input. The students' task is to make some kind of connection between their school's playground equipment and *dogwood* (the random word in this case). Each individual student or group will come up with different responses. Perhaps one youngster is inspired by the aroma of dogwood blossoms and suggests that school playground equipment be scented. Another child may be inspired by the shape of the dogwood blossom and comes up with a new playground swing set that incorporates similarly shaped seats. The teacher then selects another random word from the dictionary—for example, *concert*. The young inventors may then think of their favorite rock songs and suggest that school playground equipment might feature built in CD players for young people to enjoy their favorite music while playing on the swings or jungle gym. Random input as a creative thinking strategy provides for limitless possibilities enabling children to generate many wonderful ideas for innovative inventions.

Stage 4: Planning

An old inventor's adage says, "The definition is the solution" (Caney, 1985, p. 34). In other words, the more time inventors spend on defining and explaining what they want to accomplish, the easier it will be for them to discover a solution. With clear, well-defined objectives and a thoroughly conceptualized plan, young inventors are more likely to reach their goals. Some student inventors may not care for the planning stage of the invention process, claiming that it stifles their creativity; however, they will eventually realize the importance of writing a plan that defines and describes what they want to accomplish.

Have students spend several class sessions writing thorough plans for their products in their Inventor's Notebooks. Have them generate a list of all of the materials they will need to create their invention. Following Caney's (1985) suggestion, require that they write a business plan. The purpose of the business plan is to establish approximately how much money and time would be involved in each stage of the invention process. In addition, they will need to consider what particular skills, people, and other necessary resources will be involved. Students have to consider whether or not they will need outside assistance from an expert and whether or not they will have to finance a loan from their parents to purchase the materials needed to build their inventions. Much of the information they include in their Inventor's

Notebook will involve educated guessing and some research for resources; however, getting the students to write such a plan really forces them to think through their entire invention process from beginning to end. Inventor's Notebooks may first be filled with rough sketches and then eventually detailed drawings of how they envision their invention.

Caney (1985) explained that inventions undergo three physical stages to get from an idea to a finished product: (1) breadboard, (2) model, and (3) prototype. A breadboard is the first rough draft of an invention to determine whether or not the idea will work. It helps prove that a young inventor can take an idea and translate it into a physical device that can be successfully demonstrated. A model requires that an inventor consider choices regarding size, style, where the invention will be used, quality, and materials available for production, safety factors involved, and any special features. These concerns are important in determining how young inventors will develop their ideas into a model. Finally, the prototype is a handmade, one-of-a-kind sample made exactly like the finished product with all of the final details considered, including color, graphics, packaging, and instructions.

Students should be given time to work on their breadboards in the classroom, since they can be made from common materials. The teacher should maintain a supply of various items that might be useful to students in this initial stage of planning, such as corrugated cardboard, wire, string, yarn, heavy-duty electrical tape, Velcro strips, metal rings, small pieces of plywood, and fabric. Once students have had enough time to design several breadboards, they can pursue the design of their model and eventually the building of their final prototype at home.

Stage 5: Building

It is suggested that the building of the inventions take place at home. Send students home with their Inventor's Notebooks and a letter to their parents explaining the objectives of the unit and the plans their children have for designing an innovative product. Many parents often report that their children set up workshops in the basement or garage. Students can spread out their materials and begin tinkering according to their well-conceptualized plans drawn in their Inventor's Notebook.

Munson (2001) highlighted a number of ways that parents can help their children as "guides on the side" during the building stage. She noted that a shopping trip to a store that offers a variety of fabrics, electrical switches, wire, paint, or whatever the young inventor may need would be an appropriate and helpful parent contribution. Munson also pointed out that parents can assist their children in learning how to use specific tools or help them recruit experts who can teach them the invention-building skills they need, such as welding, sewing, or wiring.

In the letter to the parents, consider highlighting the importance of allowing children to do their own work. Assure parents that it is acceptable for them to assist with tools and anything else that might be potentially dangerous; however, the finished products should represent the authentic efforts of the young inventor. Also in the letter to parents, explain the objectives in the invention activity and how they serve to enhance creativity, problems solving, and content knowledge. The authenticity of the child's project is more important than professional-looking quality.

Stage 6: Selling the Idea

In the final stage of the process, students should be required to design an advertising campaign to sell their invention. To do this successfully, they need to first name their invention. In the *Invention Book*, Caney (1985) helped young inventors understand the significance of this part of the invention process when he advised, "Naming an invention is not all that different from naming a baby or a dog or a bicycle. It is important that you like the name, but the name of an invention also has a purpose: it must help to sell the invention" (p. 49). Caney indicated that an invention's name will help determine how people think about it and should be selected to be both appealing and memorable. Young inventors may need to understand that an invention's name may be created by using the ingredients or components of the product, such as Coca-Cola's combination of the flavorful coca leaf and sweet carbonated water. Students may also appreciate how a catchy acronym may be an easy way to name a product and help people to remember it. Young inventors will attempt to come up with melodious or catchy names.

To assist students in originating names for their inventions, follow Caney's (1985) suggestions and facilitate useful brainstorming sessions in class. In doing so, ask students to think of several words to describe the major function of their products. They can then generate a list of words they associate with that function. To further assist them in selecting good invention names, consider Caney's three simple, but thoughtful questions:

- Does the name describe the product in function or attitude?

- Will people get the impression you wish to project?

- Is the name easy to say and remember? (p. 54)

With those questions in mind, have students create several columns of brainstormed words and then combine them to make clever names such as "Pooch Protector," "Toddler ChairBib," and "Wheel-O-Meal." For example, when brainstorming the major function of a certain product, students might produce:

- keeps room neat and tidy;

- helps with storage;

- prevents clutter;

- keeps children's toys in one place; and

- helps Mom.

Brainstorming words to describe that function follows, and the young inventors might generate:

- pick up;

- gather;

- collect;

- keep stuff together;

- store;

- organize;

- arrange;

- hide away; and

- contain.

With both columns of words, students examine the possibilities, experiment with combining words from each column, and determine the name of the new invention (e.g., "Klutter Keeper"). Caney's (1985) suggestions are helpful in wrapping up the invention-naming process, and once names are selected, young inventors are ready to begin creating advertising campaigns for their products.

In teaching the students about marketing an invention,

search for expertise within the community. For example, a parent of one of your students may work in marketing or a related field and can be invited as a guest speaker on the topic of selling and promoting a product. Authentic lessons from individuals with expertise in the field can be inspirational to students.

In discussing their products, students should consider such questions as "How is your invention used?," "What problem does it solve?," "What are its special features?," and "Why would someone want a product with these special features?" In helping to determine a price for selling their inventions, students need to respond to questions such as, "What did it cost you to produce your invention?" and "What is the most someone might be willing to pay for it?" In thinking through their promotional plan, have students think about the type of person who might benefit most from their products and how they might best educate consumers about the benefits and special features of their inventions.

Finally, a marketing expert can help students consider how to make their product available to the public. Would they sell it door-to-door? At the school store? In front of the local grocery store? Students can respond to each of these critical questions in their Inventor's Notebooks. Having a lesson presented by a professional in the marketing field helps students realize that the reflective writing activity was more than just another writing assignment from their teacher, but rather a serious part of a professional inventor's process.

Having carefully thought through their promotional plans, students are now ready to begin designing their product campaigns. In doing so, young inventors may enjoy writing catchy jingles, songs, or slogans. Others may prefer to write television commercial scripts and videotape them for the unveiling of their original inventions. Still others may enjoy creating artistic posters and brochures to hand out to audiences. Today's technologically savvy students also take pleasure in creating Web pages to advertise their products.

When teaching a unit on inventing, it is common for students to ask questions about the process of getting a patent. Again, seek the expertise of professionals in the community and invite a patent attorney to the classroom to speak to students about the legal aspects of inventing.

Teachers interested in having lawyers speak on these issues may want to contact the American Bar Association to identify local patent attorneys who may be available for such a purpose. Munson (2001) indicated that some patent attorneys will review an invention and conduct a patent search for a student at a very low cost; however, the average cost of acquiring a standard patent from the government approaches $3,000. Considering this financial expense and the time investment necessary to obtain a patent, it is unlikely that most young people will want to pursue such a process; however, students will be interested in and appreciate receiving the information. It also serves to help students realize the economics involved in the invention process. Students also may enjoy reading about this process in Caney's (1985) *Invention Book*, where it is described in user-friendly terminology appropriate for young audiences.

With a guest presentation from a patent attorney and help-ful reading material from Caney (1985), young inventors are provided with the necessary introductory information they need to pursue the patent process should they want to acquire exclusive rights to sell their inventions.

Invention Conventions and Competitions

At the conclusion of an instructional unit on inventing, when students have successfully completed designing their inventions and implemented advertising campaigns, organize an invention convention.

The organizational process is similar in format to a science fair. Recruit several teachers from other schools in the school district along with outside community members to serve as judges. On the day of the convention, students demonstrate their inventions for the judges and share their advertising campaign. Judges ask the young inventors questions about their process. Students can also display their Inventor's Notebooks along with their inventions, thus enabling the judges to understand the process they went through in generating the problem to be solved, thinking through a plan to solve the problem, designing the invention, and field-testing. The judges can be provided with a simple rubric with a Likert-type scale that considers the following:

1. Does the invention solve the problem, or "bug"?

2. Does it really work?

3. Is the invention original?

4. Is the invention well designed?

5. Does the inventor's advertising campaign help to con-
    vince the buyer and "sell" the invention?

The students whose inventions are ranked the highest by
the judges can receive colorful ribbons or some other type
of award. Following the judging, students can celebrate their
success as young inventors with refreshments and have their
parents attend.

Some teachers may enjoy having their students become
involved in national invention conventions. Westberg (1998)
indicated that some states or school systems sponsor student
invention contests and exhibitions. She suggested that parents
and educators inquire within their state's department of education regarding the availability of such programs. With access
to the Internet, educators and parents can also obtain current
information on a number of excellent programs supporting
young inventors. Several well-established invention programs
designed to encourage young people as inventors sponsor
annual competitions (see the Resources section).

Whether invention conventions are at the individual classroom, school, school district, state, or national level, they hold
tremendous potential in motivating students to investigate
inventions, inventing, and inventors. Moreover, they provide
authentic outlets for young people to apply their problem-
solving skills and display their innovative talents (Flack, 1989).

Conclusion

Having taught an instructional unit on inventions and inventing to many students at various grade levels, I have had the opportunity to reflect on the benefits of such instruction for young people. Along with fostering creativity, such instruction serves as an effective method to deliver authentic thinking-skills instruction. In addition, young inventors can also be exposed to a number of professionals associated with the inventing process, which may inspire them to consider pursuing related careers in marketing or the legal profession. They have fun in the process of coming up with an idea, planning their invention, building it, and developing a marketing campaign to sell it. Through a culminating Invention Convention, they gain experience with healthy competition. Finally, the experience of trying their hand at inventing provides students with opportunities to address real problems in their lives.

It is my hope that practicing such a process will serve as an experience that has long-lasting transfer to other aspects of students' lives and enables them to continue thinking innovatively as adults.

Publications

Resources

Bellavance, T., & Bellavance, R. (1999). *Inventing made easy: The entrepreneur's indispensable guide to creating, patenting, and profiting from inventions.* Moosup, CT: Quiet Corner Press.

Gold, R. (1994). *Eureka! The entrepreneurial inventor's guide to developing, protecting, and profiting from your ideas.* Englewood Cliffs, NJ: Prentice Hall.

Resources such as these enable students to understand that inventing is a process involving years of hard work, commitment, problem solving, and creativity applied in a variety of ways.

Freeman, A., & Golden, B. (1997). *Why didn't I think of that? Bizarre origins of ingenious inventions we couldn't live without.* New York: Wiley.

Teachers will enjoy sharing accounts of how the Slinky toy was born aboard a battleship during World War II, how Velcro came from cockleburrs that got stuck on an engineer's woolen pants, how the potato chip became so popular, and how two entrepreneurial teenagers became millionaires by inventing Roller Blades. In addition, the book includes delightful stories behind games and toys that have entertained children and adults over the years such as LEGOS, the game of Trivial Pursuit, and a famous doll named Barbie.

Platt, R. (1994). *Smithsonian visual timeline of inventions*. New York: Dorling Kindersley.

Platt and his colleagues at the Smithsonian Institution have traced the history of inventions, from simple tools discovered by archaeologists studying the buried ruins of ancient Egypt, to present-day inventors designing solar-powered cars. This colorful timeline will not only captivate potential young inventors, but also mesmerize classroom history buffs with the wealth of information presented.

Wood, R. (1996). *Great inventions*. San Francisco: Weldon Owen.

Richard Wood's compilation of inventions provides students with a dynamic reference book filled with vivid photographs and helpful information on a wide variety of inventions. The inventions featured in *Great Inventions* are presented in categories, follow historical timelines, and are accompanied by delightful vignettes describing the interesting circumstances behind each's evolution.

Web Sites

Invent America!

http://www.inventamerica.com

Invent America! is a nonprofit education program for K–8 students that helps young people develop creative thinking and problem-solving skills through inventing. In the annual national contest, inventions are judged on the basis of creativity, usefulness, illustration, communication of ideas, and the background research conducted by the students. National contest winners receive generous U.S. Savings Bonds as awards, and their inventions are displayed at the Smithsonian Institution.

Invention Dimension and the Lemelson–MIT Program

http://www.inventiondimension.com

An invaluable Web resource is the Invention Dimension from the Massachusetts Institute of Technology, which offers more than 85 links to current information for young inventors and entrepreneurs. Included in the links is a connection to the Lemelson-MIT Program. Based at the Massachusetts Institute of Technology, the program was established by an independent inventor, the late James H. Lemelson and his wife, Dorothy. The program celebrates inventor and innovator success stories through outreach activities and annual awards. The program encourages students to pursue careers in science, engineering, technology, and entrepreneurship and offers the world's single largest prize for invention, the $500,000 Lemelson-MIT Prize.

National Science Teachers Association Programs

http://www.nsta.org/programs/craftsman

The National Science Teachers Association and Sears Roebuck cosponsor the Craftsman/NSTA Young Inventors

Award Program for students in grades 4–6. It spotlights inventors who have designed new tools or modifications of existing tools.

Young Inventors and Creators Program
http://scnc.lesa.k12.mi.us/~source/source_v1_n5.html#invent

This competition recognizes middle and high school students (grades 7–12) in eight areas of invention and eight areas of copyright creation. This program was started as a special project to commemorate the bicentennial of the U.S. Patent and Copyright System. The National Inventive Association and Hampshire College sponsor this competition. Contest categories include agriculture, business, environmental, health, household/food, leisure/entertainment, new technology, and transportation/travel.

References

Betts, G. T., & Kercher, J. K. (1999). *The autonomous learner model: Optimizing ability.* Greeley, CO: ALPS.

Caney, S. (1985). *Invention book.* New York: Workman.

Cramond, B. L. (2005). Fostering creative thinking. In F. A. Karnes & S. M. Bean (Eds.), *Methods and materials for teaching the gifted* (2nd ed., pp. 313–351). Waco, TX: Prufrock Press.

Davis, G. A. (2005). *Creativity is forever* (5th ed.). Dubuque, IA: Kendall/Hunt.

de Bono, E. (1992). *Serious creativity.* New York: HarperCollins.

Eberle, B. (1982). *Visual thinking: A SCAMPER tool for using imaging.* East Aurora, NY: D.O.K.

Eberle, B. (1996). *Scamper: Games for imagination development.* Waco, TX: Prufrock Press.

Erlbach, A. (1997). *The kids' invention book.* Minneapolis, MN: Lerner.

Feldhusen, J., & Britton-Kolloff, P. (1986). The Purdue three-stage enrichment model for gifted education at the elementary level. In J. S. Renzulli (Ed.), *Systems and models for developing programs for the gifted and talented* (pp. 126–152). Mansfield Center, CT: Creative Learning Press.

Flack, J. D. (1989). *Inventing, inventions and inventors: A teaching resource book.* Englewood, CO: Teachers' Ideas Press.

Goldberg, R. (1979). *The best of Rube Goldberg.* New York: Prentice Hall.

Gordon, W. J. J., & Poze, T. (1972). *Strange and familiar.* Cambridge, MA: SES Associates.

Halpern, D. F. (1996). *Thought and knowledge: An introduction to critical thinking.* Mahwah, NJ: Erlbaum.

Hertz, M. (1999). Invention. In M. A. Runco & S. R. Pritzker (Eds.), *Encyclopedia of creativity* (Vol. 2, pp. 95–102). New York: Academic Press.

Hester, J. P. (1994). *Teaching for thinking: A program for school improvement through teaching critical thinking across the curriculum.* Durham, NC: Carolina Academic Press.

Konigsburg, E. L. (1991). *Samuel Todd's book of great inventions.* New York: Atheneum.

Munson, M. (2001, March). "Guess what Mom and Dad . . . I'm going to be an inventor!" *Parenting for High Potential,* 24–25.

Murphy, J. (1978). *Weird and wacky inventions.* New York: Crown.

Osborn, A. F. (1961). *Applied imagination: Principles and procedures for creative problem solving.* New York: Charles Scribner's Sons.

Renzulli, J. S. (1999). What is this thing called giftedness, and how do we develop it?: A twenty-five year perspective. *Journal for the Education of the Gifted, 23,* 3–54.

Schlichter, C. L. (1997). Talents Unlimited Model in programs for gifted students. In N. Colangelo & G. A. Davis (Eds.), *Handbook of gifted education* (2nd ed., pp. 318–327). Boston: Allyn and Bacon.

Shlesinger, B. E. (1987). *How to invent: A text for teachers and students.* New York: IFI/Plenum.

Sobey, E. (1996). *Inventing stuff.* Palo Alto, CA: Dale Seymour.

Starko, A. J. (2001). *Creativity in the classroom: Schools of curious delight* (2nd ed.). Mawah, NJ: Erlbaum.

Taylor. B. (1987). *Be an inventor*. New York: Harcourt Brace Jovanovich.

Torrance, E. P., & Safter, H. T. (1999). *Making the creative leap beyond*. Buffalo, NY: Creative Education Foundation Press.

Westberg, K. L. (1998, September). Stimulating children's creative thinking with the invention process. *Parenting for High Potential,* 18–20, 25.

Westberg, K.L. (2002). *Teaching the invention process to students.* Instructional strand at Edufest: Summer Institute on Gifted and Talented Education, Boise State University, Boise, ID.

Thomas P. Hébert is an associate professor of educational psychology at the University of Georgia in Athens, where he teaches graduate courses in gifted and creative education and qualitative research methods. He has been a teacher for 13 years, 10 of which were spent working with gifted students at the elementary, middle, and high school levels. He serves on the board of directors of the National Association for Gifted Children (NAGC). In 2000, NAGC named Dr. Hébert an Early Scholar. Dr. Hébert conducts workshops nationally and internationally on topics related to gifted education. His areas of research interest include social and emotional development of gifted children, underachievement, culturally diverse gifted students, and problems faced by gifted young men.

Printed in the United States
by Baker & Taylor Publisher Services